I0750860

BIBLIOGRAPHY

OF THE

MASSACHUSETTS HISTORICAL SOCIETY.

BY

SAMUEL A. GREEN, M.D.

Reprinted from the Proceedings of the Massachusetts Historical Society, 1871.

BOSTON:
PRESS OF JOHN WILSON AND SON.
1871.

BIBLIOGRAPHY

OF THE

MASSACHUSETTS HISTORICAL SOCIETY.

THE first publications of the Society appeared Jan. 6, 1792, in "The American Apollo,"* a weekly magazine beginning at that time. They were printed in connection with the magazine during thirty-nine weeks, and comprised usually a signature of eight pages, which could be separated from the rest of the pamphlet, and was called Part I. of each number. The first 208 pages of Vol. I. of the Collections were published in this way; and the remainder, consisting of 80 pages, came out in monthly parts, in September, October, November, and December, 1792. The second and third volumes were continued in monthly parts, but the fourth and fifth were issued in quarterly parts. The Collections — of which there are now thirty-eight volumes — are divided into series of ten volumes each. Hubbard's History of New England, which constitutes Vols. V. and VI. of the second series, was published with a title-page to correspond with the other volumes of the Collections, — also with a different one, so that the work might be sold separately. This History passed through a second edition in 1848, when it was again printed on the same plan. This edition was carefully collated with the original manuscript, and contains numerous additional notes. The same method was followed in publishing Bradford's History of Plymouth Plantation, which is Vol. III. of the fourth series, so that it appears both as an independent volume and as one of a set. It will be seen from the list given below, that the first twenty-one volumes have been reprinted, and that Vols. I. and V. have reached a third edition.

---

* The Prospectus of this magazine reads as follows: —
To all the Friends of Science, Arts, Agriculture, Manufactures, and Commerce. Proposal of Joseph Belknap and Alexander Young, for printing a weekly paper; to be entitled THE AMERICAN APOLLO. *Containing the Publications of the* HISTORICAL SOCIETY, *Political and Commercial Intelligence, and other entertaining matter.* Printed at Boston, (*Massachusetts*) by J. Belknap and A. Young. MDCCXCI.

Vol. I. was printed in 1792, reprinted in 1806, and again reprinted in 1859.

Vol. V. was printed in 1798, reprinted in 1816, and again reprinted in 1835.

Vol.			
Vol.	II.	was printed in 1793,	and reprinted in 1810.
,,	III.	,, ,, ,, 1794,	,, ,, ,, 1810.
,,	IV.	,, ,, ,, 1795,	,, ,, ,, 1835.
,,	VI.	,, ,, ,, 1800,	,, ,, ,, 1846.
,,	VII.	,, ,, ,, 1801,	,, ,, ,, 1846.
,,	VIII.	,, ,, ,, 1802,	,, ,, ,, 1856.
,,	IX.	,, ,, ,, 1804,	,, ,, ,, 1857.
,,	X.	,, ,, ,, 1809,	,, ,, ,, 1857.

Second Series.

Vol.			
Vol.	I.	was printed in 1814,	and reprinted in 1838.
,,	II.	,, ,, ,, 1814,	,, ,, ,, 1846.
,,	III.	,, ,, ,, 1815,	,, ,, ,, 1846.
,,	IV.	,, ,, ,, 1816,	,, ,, ,, 1846.
,,	V.	,, ,, ,, 1815,	,, ,, ,, 1848.
,,	VI.	,, ,, ,, 1815,	,, ,, ,, 1848.
,,	VII.	,, ,, ,, 1818,	,, ,, ,, 1826.
,,	VIII.	,, ,, ,, 1819,	,, ,, ,, 1826.
,,	IX.	,, ,, ,, 1822,	,, ,, ,, 1832.
,,	X.	,, ,, ,, 1823,	,, ,, ,, 1843.

Third Series.

Vol.			
Vol.	I.	was printed in 1825,	and reprinted in 1846.
,,	II.	,, ,, ,, 1830.	
,,	III.	,, ,, ,, 1833.	
,,	IV.	,, ,, ,, 1834.	
,,	V.	,, ,, ,, 1836.	
,,	VI.	,, ,, ,, 1837.	
,,	VII.	,, ,, ,, 1838.	
,,	VIII.	,, ,, ,, 1843.	
,,	IX.	,, ,, ,, 1846.	
,,	X.	,, ,, ,, 1849.	

Fourth Series.

Vol.		
Vol.	I.	was printed in 1852.
,,	II.	,, ,, ,, 1854.
,,	III.	,, ,, ,, 1856.
,,	IV.	,, ,, ,, 1858.
,,	V.	,, ,, ,, 1861.
,,	VI.	,, ,, ,, 1863.
,,	VII.	,, ,, ,, 1865.
,,	VIII.	,, ,, ,, 1868.

The first volume of the Proceedings was published in 1859, and the series has been continued to the present time. These volumes comprise the proceedings of the Society, and begin with the Annual Meeting, April 12, 1855. Nine have now been published. They are not numbered on the title-pages, but have been marked on the backs of the covers with the years in which the meetings were held; for example, the first volume which ends with December, 1858, is marked 1855–1858. The last volume, for 1869–1870, has appeared in eight parts, each one, with a single exception, containing the proceedings of two meetings, or more, according to the length of the record. One hundred copies of these parts have been printed for the convenience of members. This plan gives an opportunity to detect mistakes for correction in the stereotype plates.

The first printed Catalogue of the books in the Library was a pamphlet of 40 pages, and appeared in 1796. This was followed by a "Catalogue of the Books, Pamphlets, Newspapers, Maps, Charts, Manuscripts," &c., in 1811. The first volume of the present Catalogue appeared in 1859, and the second volume was issued the next year. These three are the only printed lists of the books in the general library. A few copies of the first 240 pages of Vol. I. of the Catalogue were printed separately as specimen numbers to show to the members. It may be worth the while to put on record a fact in regard to the Catalogue of the Dowse Library. The book was printed before the Library was given to the Historical Society, and a title-page was prepared for twenty-five copies, the owner deciding to limit the issue to that number during his life. At a later period, however, the additional sheets of the catalogue were found, and it was deemed advisable to print a new title-page for the remaining copies. In the list hereafter given, it appears that there are two Catalogues of the Dowse Library, bearing the dates 1856 and 1870 respectively, though in fact they are the same work with different title-pages.

In 1869 a volume was published, entitled "Lectures delivered in a Course before the Lowell Institute, in Boston, by Members of the Massachusetts Historical Society, on Subjects relating to the Early History of Massachusetts."

This course comprised thirteen lectures, of which twelve were published in a pamphlet form by their respective authors. The following is a list of those that were thus printed: —

Massachusetts and its Early History. Introductory Lecture in the course on the Early History of Massachusetts, by Members of the Massachusetts Historical Society, at the Lowell Institute, delivered January 5, 1869. By Robert C. Winthrop. pp. 27.

I. The Aims and Purposes of the Founders of Massachusetts.
II. Their Treatment of Intruders and Dissentients.
Two Lectures, delivered January 8 and January 12, 1869. By George E. Ellis. pp. 100.

History of Grants under the Great Council for New England, delivered January 15, 1869. By Samuel F. Haven. pp. 36.

The Colony of New Plymouth and its Relations to Massachusetts, delivered January 19, 1869. By William Brigham. pp. 27.

Slavery as it once prevailed in Massachusetts, delivered January 22, 1869. By Emory Washburn. pp. 35.

Records of Massachusetts under its First Charter, delivered January 26, 1869. By Charles W. Upham. pp. 30.

The Medical Profession in Massachusetts, delivered January 29, 1869. By Oliver Wendell Holmes. pp. 45.

The Regicides sheltered in New England, delivered February 5, 1869. By Chandler Robbins. pp. 36.

The First Charter and the Early Religious Legislation of Massachusetts, delivered February 9, 1869. By Joel Parker. pp. 85.

Puritan Politics in England and New England, delivered February 12, 1869. By Edward E. Hale. pp. 22.

Education in Massachusetts, delivered February 16, 1869. By George B. Emerson. pp. 36.

The following is a list of the minor publications of the Society, and includes all papers, as far as can now be ascertained, that have been brought before it and afterward printed. They have for the most part been reprinted from the Collections, or the Proceedings. When they are not otherwise described, they are in octavo form and bear the imprint of Boston. The editions of such publications are usually limited to a small number of copies, — generally from thirty to one hundred, — and are printed for the persons most interested in them. Since 1859 it has been the custom at the Annual Meeting, for the Treasurer of the Society to give on a printed sheet a statement of the funds. But these sheets do not appear in the list.

Acts, By-Laws, &c.

Acts of Incorporation, Laws, and Circular Letter, with Appendix. 1794. pp. 14.

The Act of Incorporation, By-Laws, Catalogue of Members, and Circular Letter of the Mass. Hist. Soc. 1813. pp. 26.

Laws and Regulations of the Mass. Hist. Soc., revised and reported by the Standing Committee. Cambridge, 1833. pp. 8.

The Act of Incorporation and By-Laws. 1853. pp. 12.

The Act of Incorporation, with the Additional Acts, and By-Laws. 1857. pp. 19.

Circulars, &c.

Circular Letter of the Historical Society. [1791.] pp. 3.

Circular Letter addressed in 1794, by Jeremy Belknap, to Gentlemen of Science in America, requesting Historical Information, and Contributions to the Library and Cabinet. [No imprint.] 4to, pp. 3.

Circular Letter in relation to the Society. 1832. 4to, 1 page.

Circular Letter to the Members. 1844. 4to, 1 page.

Circular Letter to the Members. 1854. 4to, pp. 3.

Circular Letter to the Members. 1857. 4to, 1 page.

Circular Letter to the Resident and Corresponding Members, soliciting Contributions to the Library and Cabinet. [No imprint.] 4to, pp. 3.

Circular relating to the Collection of Memorials of the War. August 8, 1861. 4to, 1 page.

Circular to Members relating to Photographs. February 15, 1865. 12mo, 1 page.

Circular relating to the Publications of the Society, with Table of Contents. [1865.] 4to, pp. 4.

Prospectus for Hubbard's History of New England. [1814.]

Prospectus for the Historical Collections. 1814.

Prospectus for the Proceedings for 1855–58. 1859.

Prospectus for the Lectures on the Early History of Massachusetts. 1869.

Prospectus for the Sewall Diary 1870.

Notification of an election of a member, with a Circular soliciting Contributions to the Library and Cabinet. [No imprint.] 4to, pp. 3.

List of Resident Members. June, 1864. Folio, 1 page.

MEMOIRS, TRIBUTES, &c.

Memoir towards a Character of John Eliot. [By Joseph McKean.] 1793. pp. 40.

Notices of the Life of Benjamin Lincoln. [1815.] pp. 23.

[This paper is signed P. C. It is accredited, however, in the Index of Authors, to John T. Kirkland. Vol. X., 2d Series, pp. 201.]

Memoir of Wiliam Tudor. [By William Tudor, Jr.] 1826. pp. 41.

Biographical Notice of Dudley A. Tyng. By John Lowell. [No imprint.] pp. 17.

Memoir of John Allyn. By Convers Francis. [1836.] pp. 8.

Memoir of John Pickering. By William H. Prescott. Cambridge, 1848. pp. 27.

Memoir of Thaddeus Mason Harris. By Nathaniel L. Frothingham. 1854. pp. 28.

Memoir of Abbott Lawrence. By Nathan Appleton. 1856. pp. 21.

Memoir of William P. Lunt. By Nathaniel L. Frothingham. [No imprint.] pp. 8.

The Same. Privately printed. 1858. pp. 16.

Memoir of William Appleton. By Chandler Robbins. 1863. pp. 64.

Memoir of Nathan Appleton. By Robert C. Winthrop. 1861. pp. 79.

Memoir of Luther V Bell. By George E. Ellis. 1863. pp. 75.

Memoir of Charles Mason. By A. P. Peabody. [With an appendix.] 1863. pp. 39.

Memoir of William Sturgis. By Charles G. Loring. 1864. pp. 64.

Memoir of Josiah Quincy. By James Walker. Cambridge, 1867. pp. 76.

Memoir of Joseph Willard. Cambridge, 1867. pp. 25.

Memoir of Joseph Story. By George S. Hillard. 1868. pp. 32.

Memoir of George Livermore. By Charles Deane. Cambridge, 1869. pp. 60.

Memoir of Jared Sparks. By George E. Ellis. Cambridge, 1869. pp. 106.

The Same. [50 copies printed on large paper.]

Memoir of Levi Lincoln. By Emory Washburn. Cambridge, 1869. pp. 39.

Memoir of Charles Greely Loring. By Theophilus Parsons. Cambridge, 1870. pp. 31.

Memoir of Nathaniel L. Frothingham. By Frederic H. Hedge. 1870. pp. 20.

Proceedings of the Mass. Hist. Soc. in respect to the memory of William Hickling Prescott, February 1, 1859. 1859. pp. 53.

Tribute of the Mass. Hist. Soc. to the memory of Josiah Quincy, July 14, 1864. 1864. pp. 32.

[Tribute by the President to Benjamin Silliman and Charles Christian Rafn. 1864. pp. 4.]

Tribute of the Mass. Hist. Soc. to the memory of Edward Everett, January 30, 1865. 1865. pp. 90.

Tribute of the Mass. Hist. Soc. to the memory of George Livermore. 1866. pp. 19.

Tribute to Henry H. Milman. [1868.] pp. 4.

Tribute to John Pendleton Kennedy. [1870.] pp. 16.

Dowse Library.

Catalogue of the Private Library of Thomas Dowse. Presented to the Mass. Hist. Soc., July 30, 1856. [Twenty-five copies printed.] 1856. pp. 214.

The Same. 1870. pp. 214.

Report of the Proceedings at the Annual Meeting, on the presentation of the Dowse Library, April 9, 1857. pp. 8.

Eulogy on Thomas Dowse, of Cambridgeport, pronounced before the Mass. Hist. Soc., December 9, 1858, by Edward Everett, with the Introductory Address of Mr. Winthrop, and an Appendix. 1859. pp. 82.

Proceedings of the Mass. Hist. Soc., relating to the donations from Thomas Dowse; with Eulogy of Edward Everett. Privately printed. 1859. pp. 80.

Miscellaneous.

A Discourse intended to commemorate the Discovery of America by Columbus. Delivered at the request of the Historical Society in Massachusetts, October 23, 1792. With Four Dissertations connected with various parts of the Discourse. By Jeremy Belknap. 1792. pp. 132.

Historical Journal of the American War. [By Thomas Pemberton.] 1795. pp. 304.

Description and History of Newton, in the County of Middlesex. By Jonathan Homer. [1798.] pp. 28.

The History of Cambridge. By Abiel Holmes. 1801. pp. 67.

A Memoir of the Moheagan Indians. [By Abiel Holmes. 1804.] pp. 27.

A Memoir of Stephen Parmenius, of Buda; with a Latin Poem, &c. [By Abiel Holmes. 1804.] pp. 19.

Order of Services, December 22, 1813, at King's Chapel, Boston, in Commemoration of the Landing of the Forefathers. 1813. pp. 4.

A Discourse before the Mass. Hist. Soc., Boston, December 22, 1813, at the Annual Commemoration of the First Landing at Plymouth, 1620. By John Davis. 1814. pp. 31.

Annals of New England. By Thomas Prince. Vol. II. Nos. I.–III. 1818. pp. 97.

A Memoir of the French Protestants, who settled at Oxford, in Massachusetts, 1686, with a Sketch of the Entire History of the Protestants in France. By Abiel Holmes. Cambridge, 1826. pp. 84.

Vocabulary of the Massachusetts Indian Language. By Josiah Cotton. Cambridge, 1829. pp. 112.

List of Portraits in the Hall of the Historical Society. [1838.] pp. 285–292.

[Regulations of the] Library of the Mass. Hist. Soc., April, 1841. pp. 2.

The New England Confederacy of 1643. A Discourse delivered before the Mass. Hist. Soc., May 29, 1843. By John Quincy Adams. 1843. pp. 47.

Memoirs of the Pilgrims at Leyden. By George Sumner. Cambridge, 1845. pp. 35.

The first Plymouth Patent, granted June 1, 1621. Edited by Charles Deane. Privately printed. Cambridge, 1854. pp. 16.

Proceedings of the Mass. Hist. Soc. [An account of the Annual Meeting, April 12.] 1855. pp. 15.

Washington chair presented to the Mass. Hist. Soc., by Benjamin R. Winthrop. [1856.] pp. 7.

A Bibliographical Essay on Governor Hutchinson's Historical Publications. By Charles Deane. . . . 1857. pp. 39. Fifty copies privately printed.

Memorial of the Mass. Hist. Soc. to the Legislature. [1858.] 4to, pp. 3.

Speech of Josiah Quincy before a Committee of the Legislature, February, 1858. pp. 8.

A Declaration of the Affairs of the English People that first inhabited New England. By Phinehas Pratt. Edited with notes, by Richard Frothingham, Jr. 1858. pp. 20.

Paper read before the Mass. Hist. Soc., January, 1859 [on the uniform of the Continental Army]. By C. H. Warren. pp. 6.

Proceedings of the Mass. Hist. Soc. 1858–1860. Selected from the Records. [Specimen.] 1859. pp. 21.

Naturalization in the American Colonies, with more particular reference to Massachusetts. By Joseph Willard. 1859. pp. 30.

Report of a Committee on Papers read at the Meetings of the Society. 1860. 4to, pp. 2.

Report of a Committee appointed by the Mass. Hist. Soc., on Exchange of Prisoners during the Revolutionary War. [By George T. Curtis.] 1861. pp. 26.

An Historical Research respecting the Opinions of the Founders of the Republic, on Negroes as Slaves, as Citizens, and as Soldiers. By George Livermore. 1862. pp. 215.

Supplementary Notes and Index to be added to the First Edition of "An Historical Research." [1862.] pp. 217–236.

An Historical Research, &c. Second edition. 1862. pp. 236.

The Same. Third edition. Published for the New England Loyal Publication Society. 1863. pp. 184.

The Same. Fourth edition. 1863. pp. 184.

The Same. Fifth edition, fifty copies on large paper. 1863. pp. 184.

Remarks on the Narraganset Patent, June, 1862. By Thomas Aspinwall. 1863. pp. 41.

The Same. Providence, 1865. pp. 40.

Plan for the General Arrangement of the Militia of the United States. By General Knox . . . with remarks by Joseph Willard. 1863. pp. 42.

List of the Maps of Boston. By Nathaniel B. Shurtleff. 1863. pp. 8.

Letters of Phillis Wheatley, the Negro-slave Poet of Boston. Privately printed. [Edited by Charles Deane.] 1864. pp. 19.

"Journal de Castorland." By John Appleton. 1864. pp. 15.

Notices of the Triennial and Annual Catalogues of Harvard University: with a reprint of the Catalogues of 1674, 1682, and 1700. By John Langdon Sibley. 1865. pp. 67.

The Same. Thirty copies on large paper.

The Origin and Sources of the Bill of Rights declared in the Constitution of Massachusetts. By Emory Washburn. Cambridge, 1866. pp. 22.

Letters of John Andrews, of Boston, 1772–1776. Compiled and edited by Winthrop Sargent. Cambridge, 1866. pp. 100.

(A list of *errata* in these letters appears in the Proceedings for 1864–1865.)

The Origin, Organization, and Influence of the Towns of New England; a paper read before the Mass. Hist. Soc., Dec. 14, 1865. By Joel Parker. Cambridge, 1867. pp. 54.

Notes concerning Peter Pelham, the earliest Artist resident in New England, and his Successors prior to the Revolution. By William H. Whitmore. Cambridge, 1867. pp. 31.

Sermon preached at Boston, in New England, upon a Fast Day, the 19th of January, 1636–37. By John Wheelwright. [With a Prefatory Note by Charles Deane.] Cambridge, 1867. pp. 22.

The Same. With notes by Henry B. Dawson. Morrisania, N. Y. 1867. pp. 28.

History of Bacon's and Ingram's Rebellion in Virginia, 1675 and 1676. [With a Prefatory Note by Charles Deane.] Cambridge, 1867. pp. 50.

John Sullivan. A Vindication of his Character as a Soldier and a Patriot. By Thomas C. Amory. Morrisania, N. Y. 1867. pp. 52.

Last Will and Testament of Capt. John Smith, with some additional memoranda relating to him. [Edited by Charles Deane.] 1867. 4to, pp. 7.

Seal of the "Council for New England." By Charles Deane. [1867.] pp. 4.

[Resolutions of the Society relating to the bust of George Peabody. 1868.] page 1.

Harvard College Monitor's Bill. Communication addressed to Mr. J. L. Sibley, from Mr. Franklin Bowditch Dexter, of Yale College. [1868.] pp. 6.

The Forms in issuing Letters-Patent by the Crown of England. By Charles Deane. Privately printed. Cambridge, 1870. pp. 24.

Life of Thomas Dudley, written as is supposed by Cotton Mather. Edited by Charles Deane. 1870. pp. 20.

Description of a Selection of Coins and Medals relating to America, exhibited to the Mass. Hist. Soc., April 28, 1870. By William S. Appleton. Cambridge, 1870. pp. 16.

"The St. Regis Bell." [By Geo. T. Davis. 1870.] pp. 311–321.

Letter written from San Francisco, Cal., to the Mass. Hist. Soc. By Robert C. Waterston. Cambridge, 1870. pp. 10.

A Dialogue or Third Conference between some Young Men born in New England, and some Ancient Men which came out of Holland and Old England, concerning the Church and the Government thereof. By William Bradford. Edited, with a preface and notes, by Charles Deane. 1870. pp. 78.

Bibliography of the Massachusetts Historical Society. By Samuel A. Green. 1871. pp. 10.

www.ingramcontent.com/pod-product-compliance
Lightning Source LLC
LaVergne TN
LVHW020639110826
845149LV00004B/1277

* 9 7 8 1 4 1 8 1 9 0 3 3 0 *